Quick Student Workbook

Study Guide
Student Workbook for
Alice's Adventures in Wonderland

By: John Pennington

The Quick Student Workbooks are designed to get students thinking critically about the text they read and providing a guided study format to facilitate in improved learning and retention. Teachers and Homeschool Instructors may use them to improve student learning and organization.

Students will construct and identify the following areas of knowledge.

Character Identification

Events

Location

Vocabulary

Main Idea

Conflict

And more as appropriate to the text.

This is a workbook for students to determine the above areas. This is not a study guide, cliff notes, or Teacher's guide.

How to use this workbook

1. Complete as many entries as possible for each chapter.
2. Not all spaces need to be filled, move on when you have exhausted the information for the chapter.
3. Complete the Review page at the end to bring the information together.
4. Notes Pages are located after the Chapter Pages. Use them to record any information not covered in the Chapter Pages.
5. Notes on the author can be kept on pages 4 and 5.

Need a Teachers Guide created?

Upgrade to the <u>Lessons on Demand</u> line of books!

Send requests and questions to Johndavidpennington@yahoo.com

Author Notes

Author Notes

Before Reading Questions

What is the reason for reading this book?

What do you already know about this book?

What, based on the cover, do you think this book is about?

Before Reading Questions

Have you read any other books by this author?

Is this book part of a series? If so what are the other books?

What are you looking forward to when reading this book?

* After Reading questions can be found in the back.

NAME:

TEACHER:

Date:

Chapter

Locations

1.
2.
3.
4.
5.

* <u>Not all number lines will have answers.</u>

Characters

1.
2.
3.
4.
5.
6.
7.
8.
9.
10.
11.
12.
13.
14.
15.
16.

Conflicts / Problems

1.
2.
3.
4.
5.
6.
7.
8.
9.
10.
11.
12.

NAME:

TEACHER:

Continued

Date:

Events

1.
2.
3.
4.
5.
6.
7.
8.
9.
10.

Main Idea

Key Terms / Vocabulary

1.
2.
3.
4.
5.
6.
7.
8.
9.
10.
11.
12.

Possible Future Events

1.
2.
3.
4.
5.
6.

NAME:

TEACHER:

Date:

Advertisement: Draw an advertisement for the book

NAME:

TEACHER:

Continued

Date:

Chapter to Poem

Assignment: Select 20 words found in the chapter to create a poem where each line is 3 words long.

Title:

_____ _____ _____

_____ _____ _____

_____ _____ _____

_____ _____ _____

_____ _____ _____

NAME:

TEACHER:

Date:

Chapter

Locations

1.
2.
3.
4.
5.

Not all number lines will have answers.

Characters

1.
2.
3.
4.
5.
6.
7.
8.
9.
10.
11.
12.
13.
14.
15.
16.

Conflicts / Problems

1.
2.
3.
4.
5.
6.
7.
8.
9.
10.
11.
12.

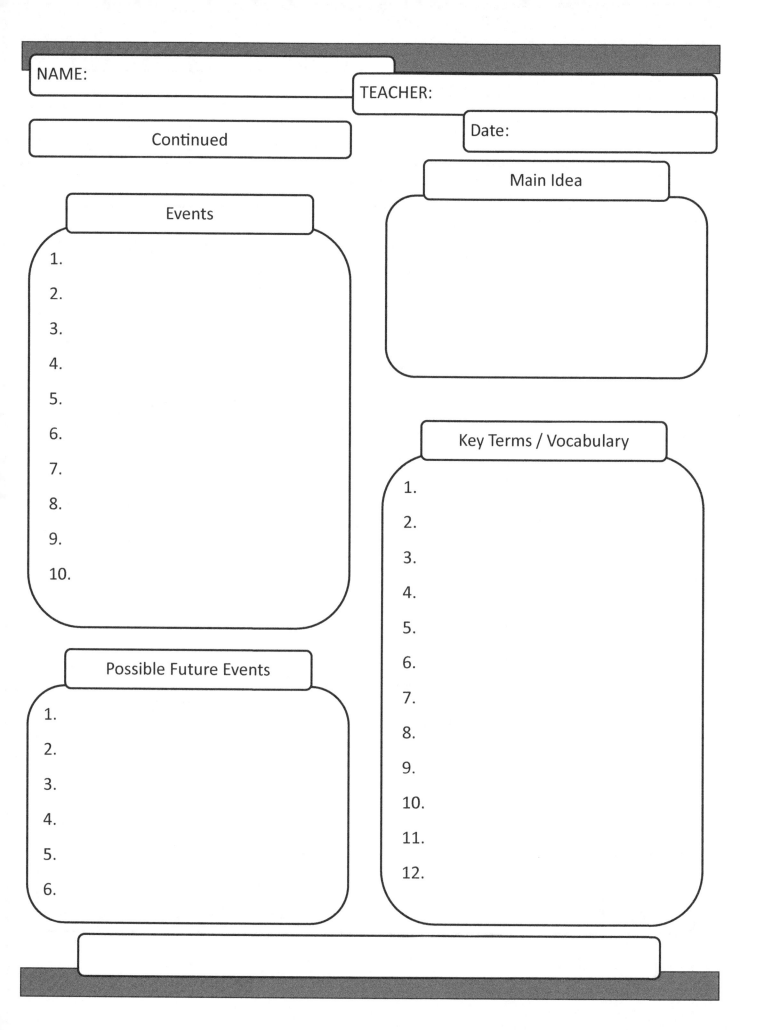

NAME:

TEACHER:

Date:

Precognition Sheet

Who ?

What's going to happen?

What will be the result?

Who ?

What's going to happen?

What will be the result?

Who ?

What's going to happen?

What will be the result?

Who ?

What's going to happen?

What will be the result?

How many did you get correct?

NAME:

TEACHER:

Date:

Who, What, When, Where, and How

Who

What

Where

When

How

NAME:

TEACHER:

Date:

Chapter

Locations

* Not all number lines will have answers.

1.
2.
3.
4.
5.

Characters

1.
2.
3.
4.
5.
6.
7.
8.
9.
10.
11.
12.
13.
14.
15.
16.

Conflicts / Problems

1.
2.
3.
4.
5.
6.
7.
8.
9.
10.
11.
12.

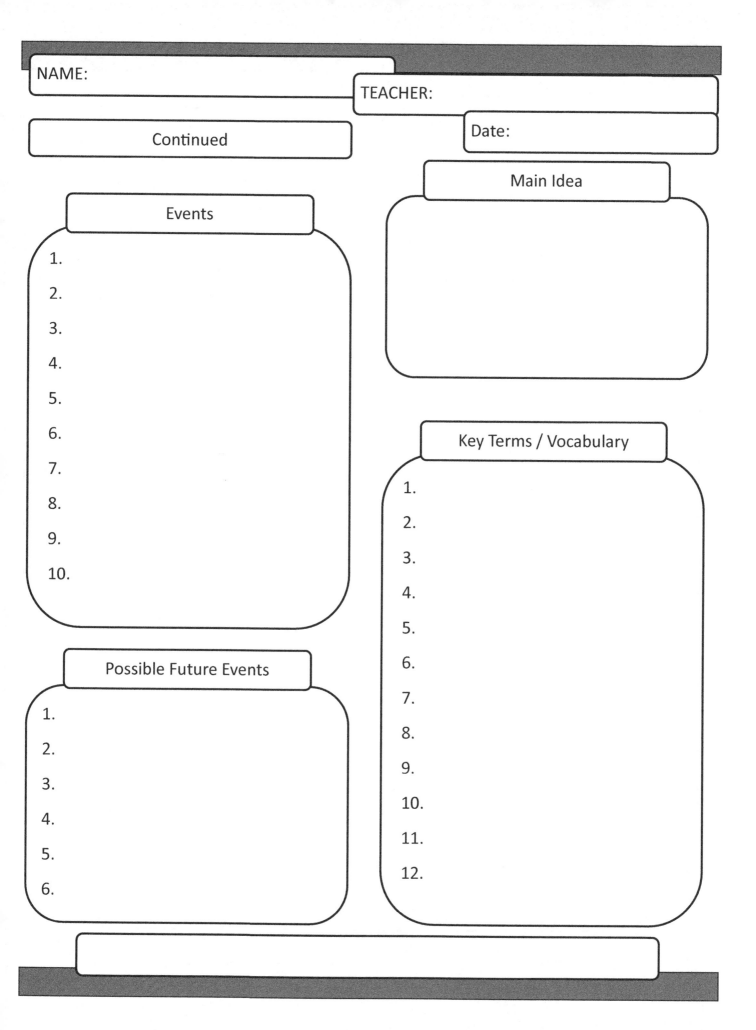

NAME:

TEACHER:

Date:

Draw the Scene: What five things have you included in the scene?

1   2   3

4   5

NAME:

TEACHER:

Date:

Interview: Who _____

Question:

Answer:

Question:

Answer:

Question:

Answer:

Question:

Answer:

NAME:

TEACHER:

Date:

Chapter

Locations

1.
2.
3.
4.
5.

Not all number lines will have answers.

Characters

1.
2.
3.
4.
5.
6.
7.
8.
9.
10.
11.
12.
13.
14.
15.
16.

Conflicts / Problems

1.
2.
3.
4.
5.
6.
7.
8.
9.
10.
11.
12.

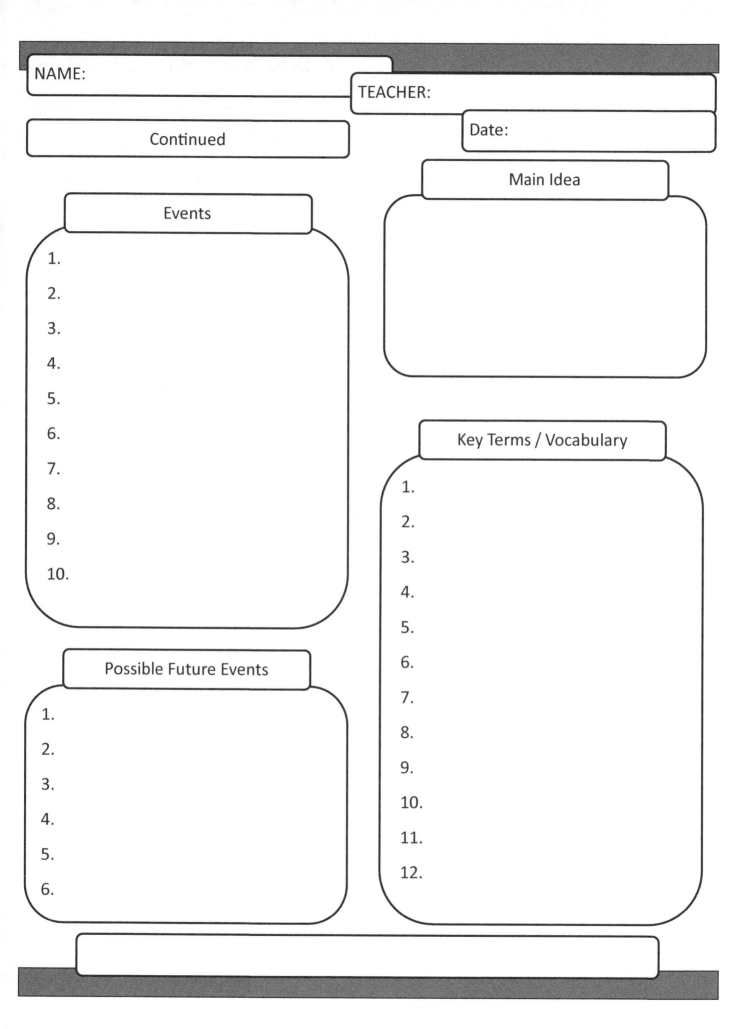

NAME:

TEACHER:

Date:

Chapter

Locations
1.
2.
3.
4.
5.

Not all number lines will have answers.

Characters
1.
2.
3.
4.
5.
6.
7.
8.
9.
10.
11.
12.
13.
14.
15.
16.

Conflicts / Problems
1.
2.
3.
4.
5.
6.
7.
8.
9.
10.
11.
12.

NAME:

TEACHER:

Continued

Date:

Main Idea

Events

1.
2.
3.
4.
5.
6.
7.
8.
9.
10.

Key Terms / Vocabulary

1.
2.
3.
4.
5.
6.
7.
8.
9.
10.
11.
12.

Possible Future Events

1.
2.
3.
4.
5.
6.

NAME:

TEACHER:

Date:

Chapter

Locations

1.
2.
3.
4.
5.

* Not all number lines will have answers.

Characters

1.
2.
3.
4.
5.
6.
7.
8.
9.
10.
11.
12.
13.
14.
15.
16.

Conflicts / Problems

1.
2.
3.
4.
5.
6.
7.
8.
9.
10.
11.
12.

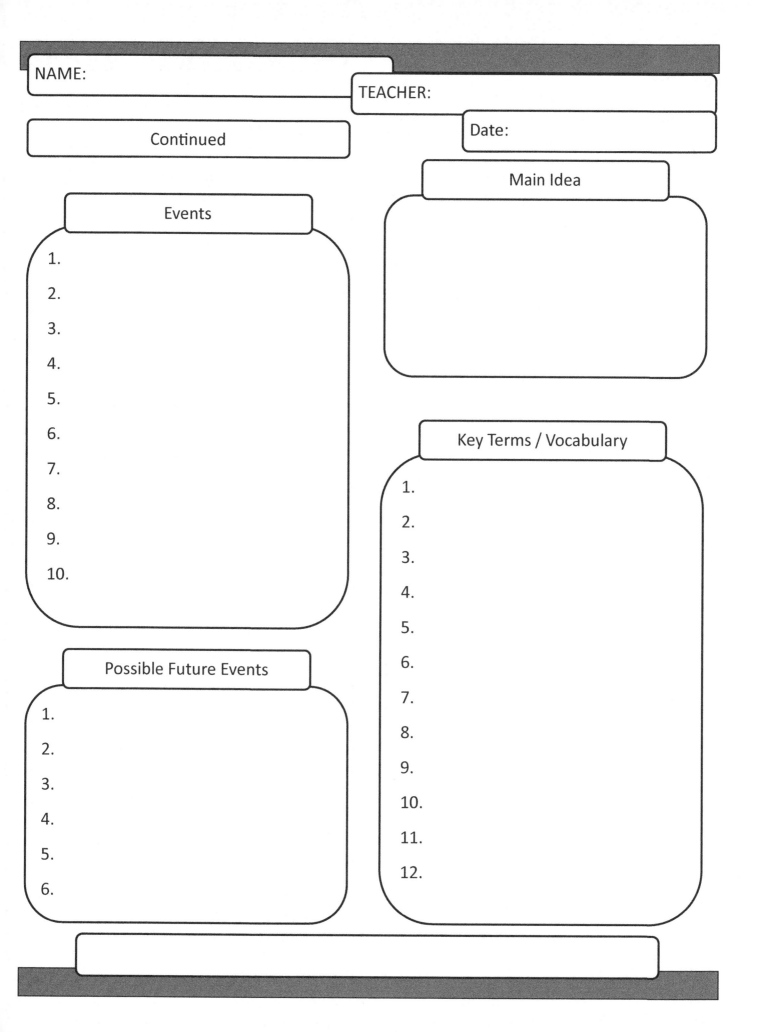

NAME:

TEACHER:

Date:

Chapter

Locations
1.
2.
3.
4.
5.

* Not all number lines will have answers.

Characters
1.
2.
3.
4.
5.
6.
7.
8.
9.
10.
11.
12.
13.
14.
15.
16.

Conflicts / Problems
1.
2.
3.
4.
5.
6.
7.
8.
9.
10.
11.
12.

NAME:

TEACHER:

Continued

Date:

Main Idea

Events

1.
2.
3.
4.
5.
6.
7.
8.
9.
10.

Key Terms / Vocabulary

1.
2.
3.
4.
5.
6.
7.
8.
9.
10.
11.
12.

Possible Future Events

1.
2.
3.
4.
5.
6.

NAME:

TEACHER:

Date:

Chapter

Locations

1.
2.
3.
4.
5.

Not all number lines will have answers.

Characters

1.
2.
3.
4.
5.
6.
7.
8.
9.
10.
11.
12.
13.
14.
15.
16.

Conflicts / Problems

1.
2.
3.
4.
5.
6.
7.
8.
9.
10.
11.
12.

NAME:

TEACHER:

Continued

Date:

Main Idea

Events

1.
2.
3.
4.
5.
6.
7.
8.
9.
10.

Key Terms / Vocabulary

1.
2.
3.
4.
5.
6.
7.
8.
9.
10.
11.
12.

Possible Future Events

1.
2.
3.
4.
5.
6.

NAME:

TEACHER:

Date:

Chapter

Not all number lines will have answers.

Characters

1.
2.
3.
4.
5.
6.
7.
8.
9.
10.
11.
12.
13.
14.
15.
16.

Locations

1.
2.
3.
4.
5.

Conflicts / Problems

1.
2.
3.
4.
5.
6.
7.
8.
9.
10.
11.
12.

NAME:

TEACHER:

Continued

Date:

Main Idea

Events

1.
2.
3.
4.
5.
6.
7.
8.
9.
10.

Key Terms / Vocabulary

1.
2.
3.
4.
5.
6.
7.
8.
9.
10.
11.
12.

Possible Future Events

1.
2.
3.
4.
5.
6.

NAME:

TEACHER:

Date:

Chapter

Locations

1.
2.
3.
4.
5.

* Not all number lines will have answers.

Characters

1.
2.
3.
4.
5.
6.
7.
8.
9.
10.
11.
12.
13.
14.
15.
16.

Conflicts / Problems

1.
2.
3.
4.
5.
6.
7.
8.
9.
10.
11.
12.

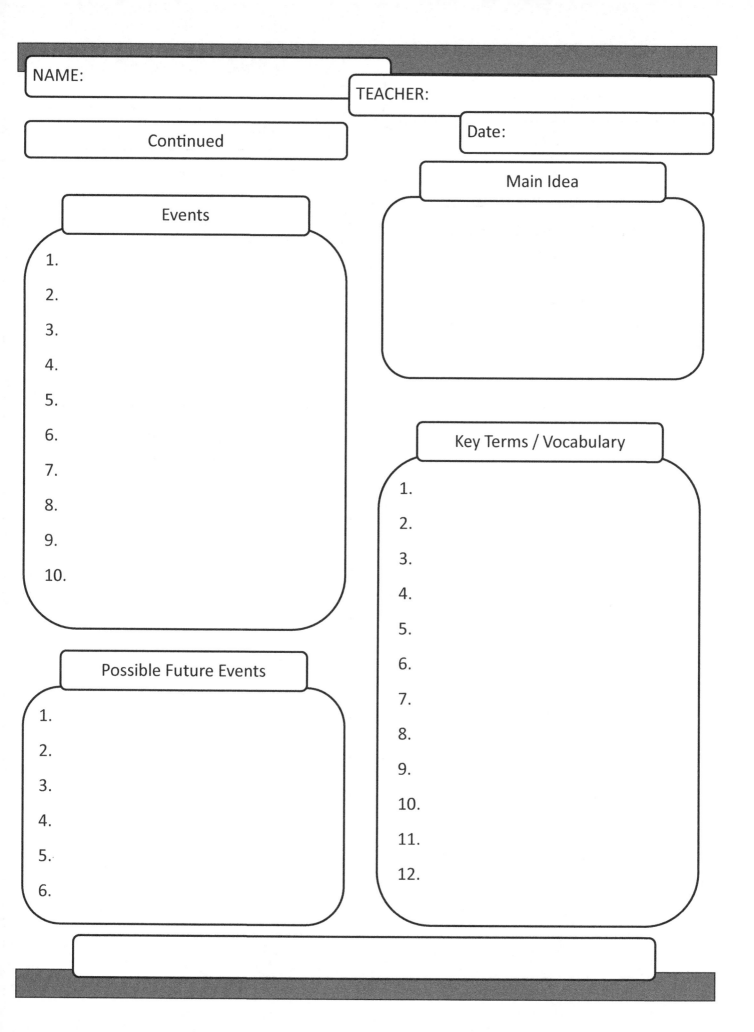

NAME:

TEACHER:

Date:

Chapter

Locations

* Not all number lines will have answers.

Characters

1.
2.
3.
4.
5.

1.
2.
3.
4.
5.
6.
7.
8.
9.
10.
11.
12.
13.
14.
15.
16.

Conflicts / Problems

1.
2.
3.
4.
5.
6.
7.
8.
9.
10.
11.
12.

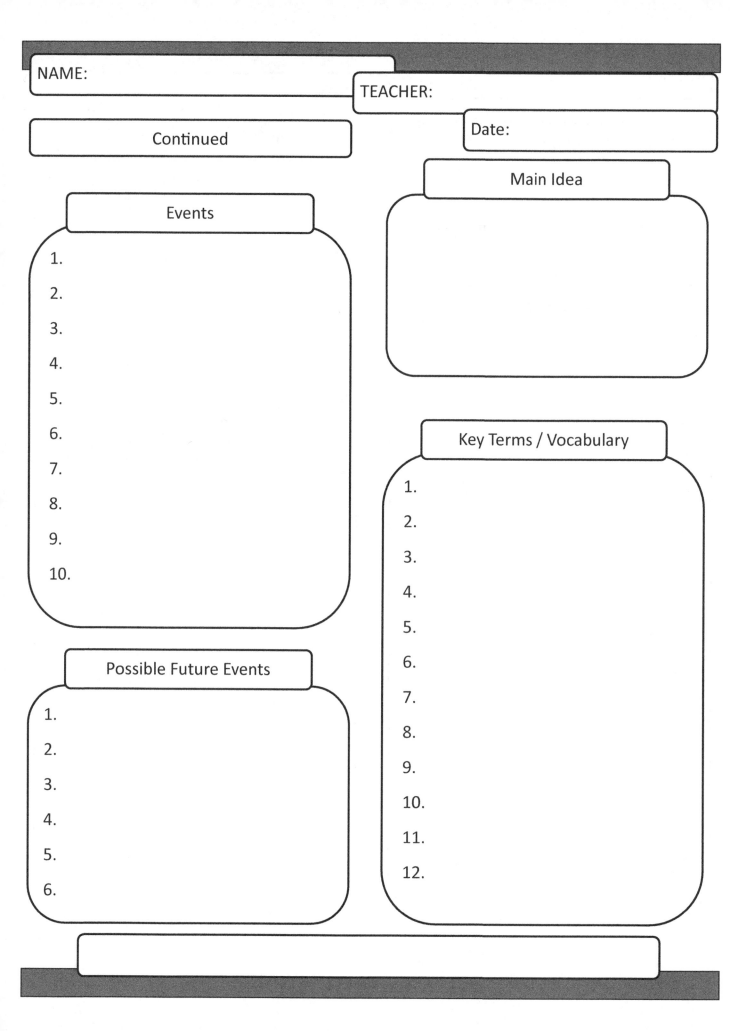

NAME:

TEACHER:

Date:

Chapter

Locations

* Not all number lines will have answers.

Characters

1.
2.
3.
4.
5.

1.
2.
3.
4.
5.
6.
7.
8.
9.
10.
11.
12.
13.
14.
15.
16.

Conflicts / Problems

1.
2.
3.
4.
5.
6.
7.
8.
9.
10.
11.
12.

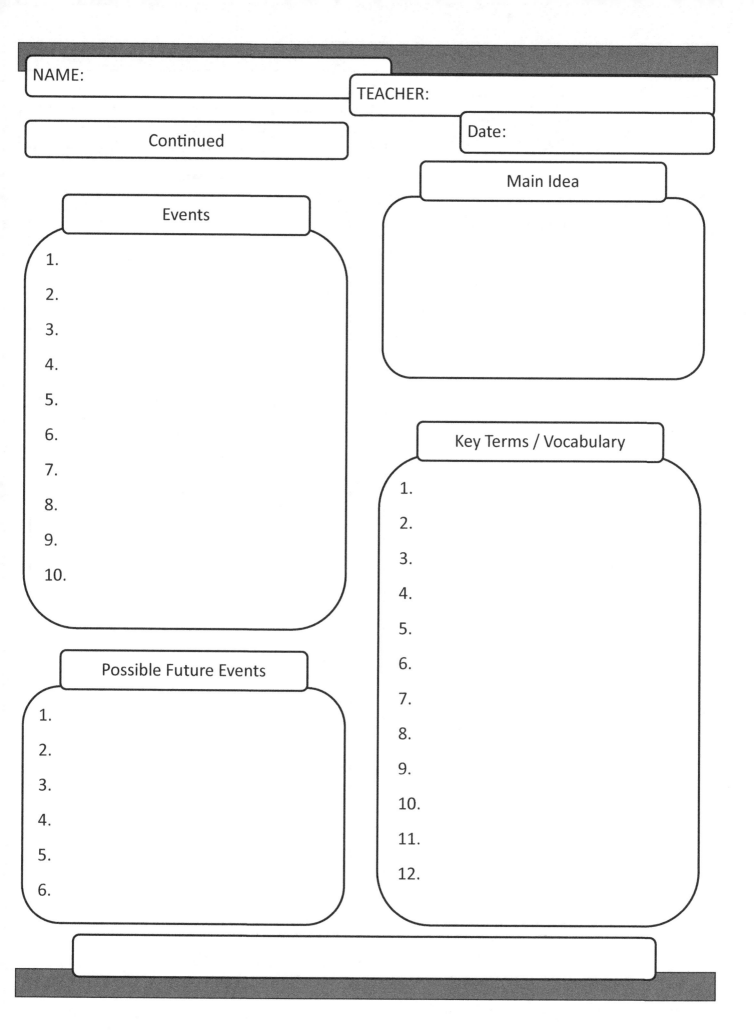

NAME:

TEACHER:

Date:

Chapter

Not all number lines will have answers.

Locations
1.
2.
3.
4.
5.

Characters
1.
2.
3.
4.
5.
6.
7.
8.
9.
10.
11.
12.
13.
14.
15.
16.

Conflicts / Problems
1.
2.
3.
4.
5.
6.
7.
8.
9.
10.
11.
12.

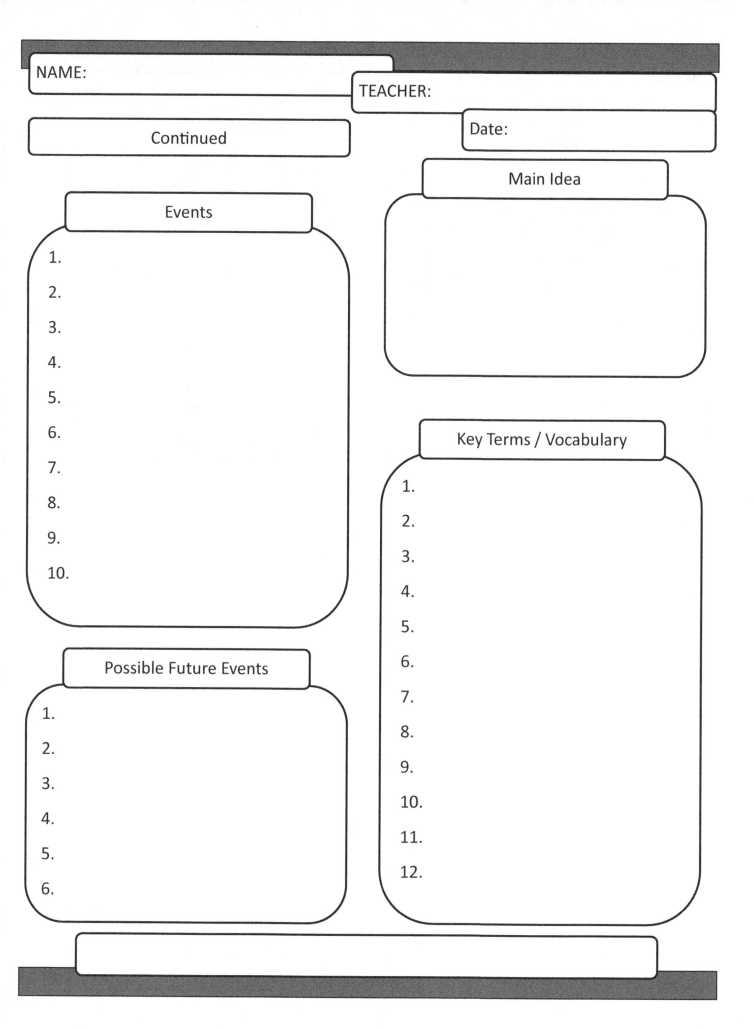

NAME:

TEACHER:

Date:

Chapter

Locations

1.
2.
3.
4.
5.

* **Not all number lines will have answers.**

Characters

1.
2.
3.
4.
5.
6.
7.
8.
9.
10.
11.
12.
13.
14.
15.
16.

Conflicts / Problems

1.
2.
3.
4.
5.
6.
7.
8.
9.
10.
11.
12.

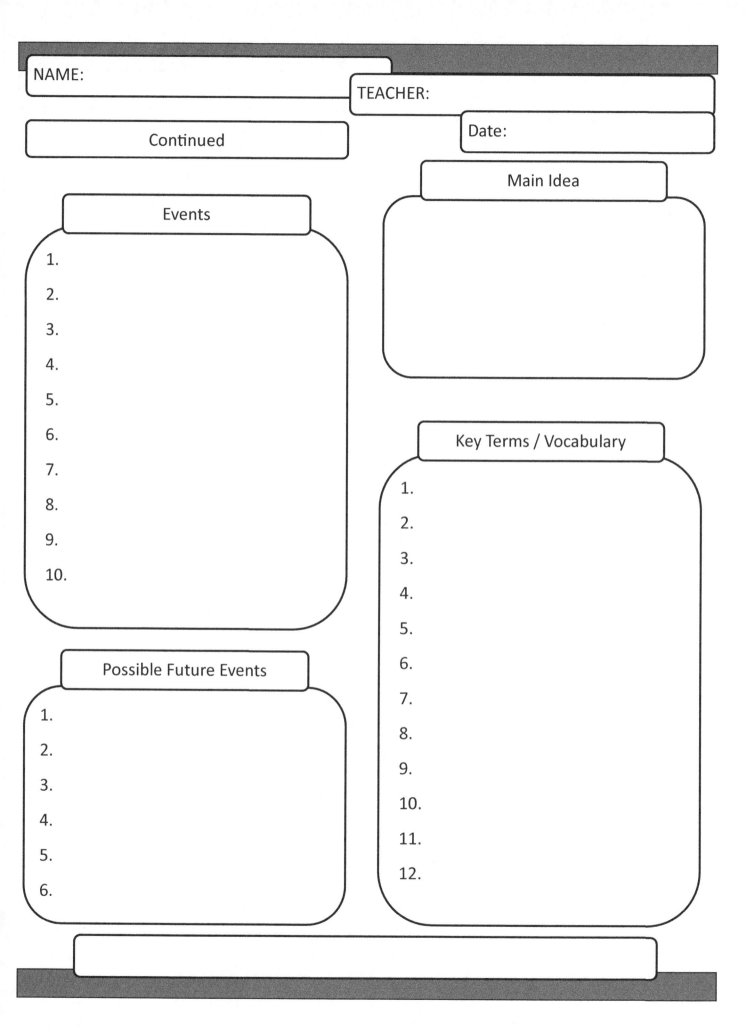

NAME:

TEACHER:

Date:

Chapter

Locations

1.
2.
3.
4.
5.

Not all number lines will have answers.

Characters

1.
2.
3.
4.
5.
6.
7.
8.
9.
10.
11.
12.
13.
14.
15.
16.

Conflicts / Problems

1.
2.
3.
4.
5.
6.
7.
8.
9.
10.
11.
12.

NAME:

TEACHER:

Continued

Date:

Main Idea

Events

1.
2.
3.
4.
5.
6.
7.
8.
9.
10.

Key Terms / Vocabulary

1.
2.
3.
4.
5.
6.
7.
8.
9.
10.
11.
12.

Possible Future Events

1.
2.
3.
4.
5.
6.

NAME:

TEACHER:

Date:

Chapter

Not all number lines will have answers.

Locations
1.
2.
3.
4.
5.

Characters
1.
2.
3.
4.
5.
6.
7.
8.
9.
10.
11.
12.
13.
14.
15.
16.

Conflicts / Problems
1.
2.
3.
4.
5.
6.
7.
8.
9.
10.
11.
12.

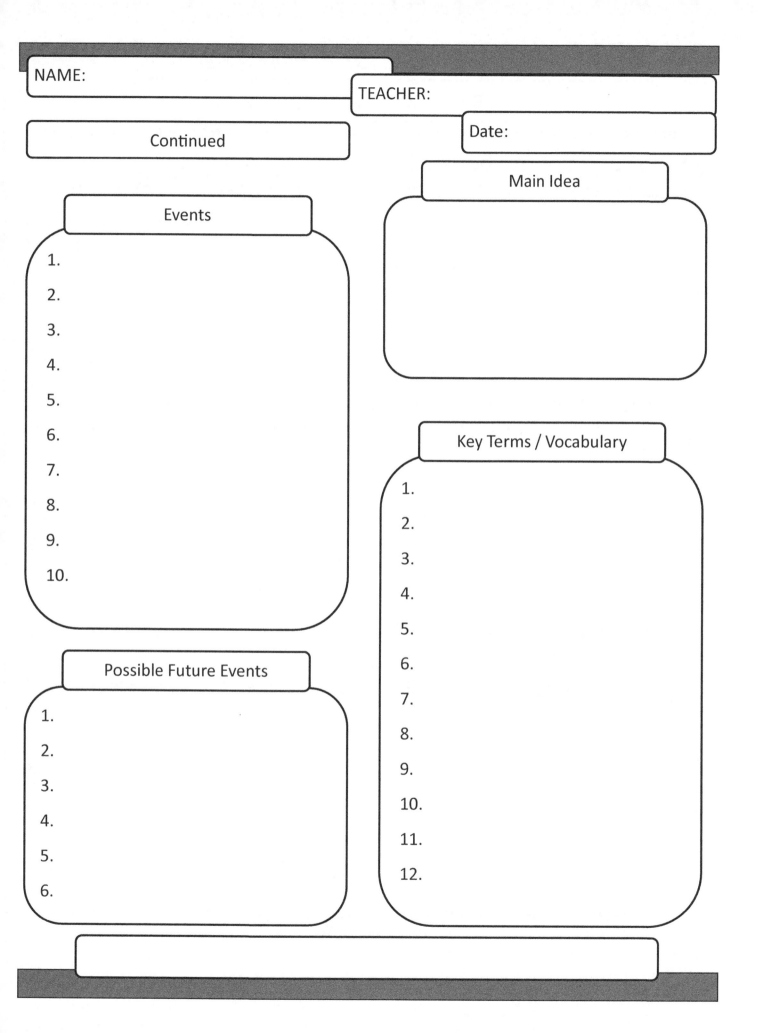

Before Reading Questions

What parts of the book were the most enjoyable?

Which characters were your favorite and why?

Write a summary of the book.

Before Reading Questions

What are the 5 most important events?

Write a review of the book.

What is likely to be a plot to the next book?

Draw an advertisement for the book

Character Sketch

Name

Personality/ Distinguishing marks

Draw a picture

Connections to other characters

Important Actions

Character Sketch

Name

Personality/ Distinguishing marks

Draw a picture

Connections to other characters

Important Actions

Character Sketch

Name

Personality/ Distinguishing marks

Draw a picture

Connections to other characters

Important Actions

Character Sketch

Name

Personality/ Distinguishing marks

Draw a picture

Connections to other characters

Important Actions

Character Sketch

Name

Personality/ Distinguishing marks

Draw a picture

Connections to other characters

Important Actions

Compare and Contrast Venn Diagram

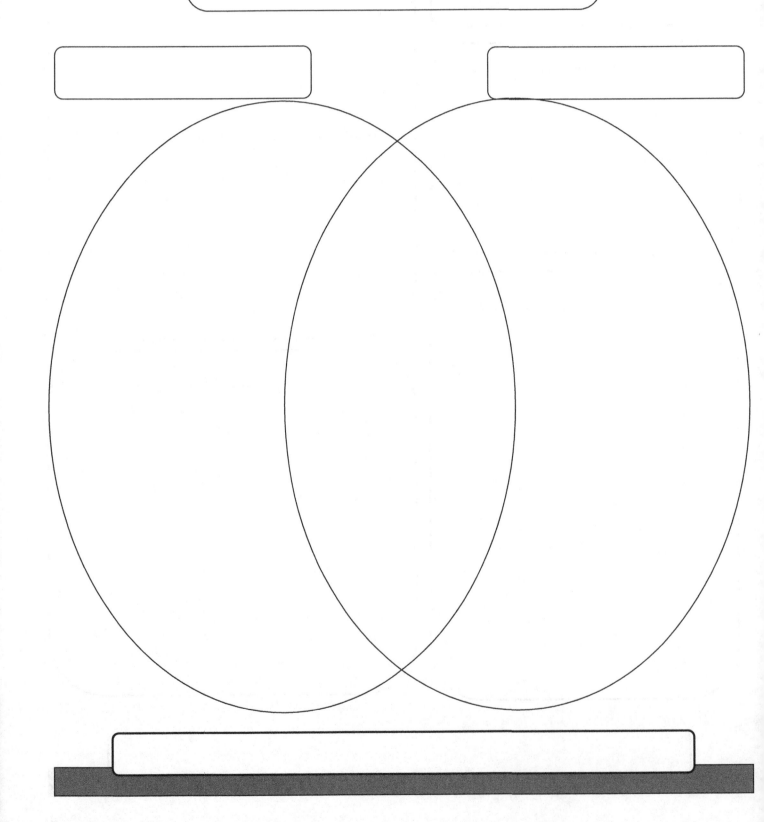

Notes

Notes

NAME:

TEACHER:

Date:

Not all number lines will have answers.

Main Characters
1.
2.
3.
4.
5.
6.
7.
8.
9.
10.
11.
12.
13.
14.
15.
16.
17.
18.

Important Locations
1.
2.
3.
4.
5.

Resolved Conflicts / Problems
1.
2.
3.
4.
5.
6.
7.
8.
9.
10.
11.
12.

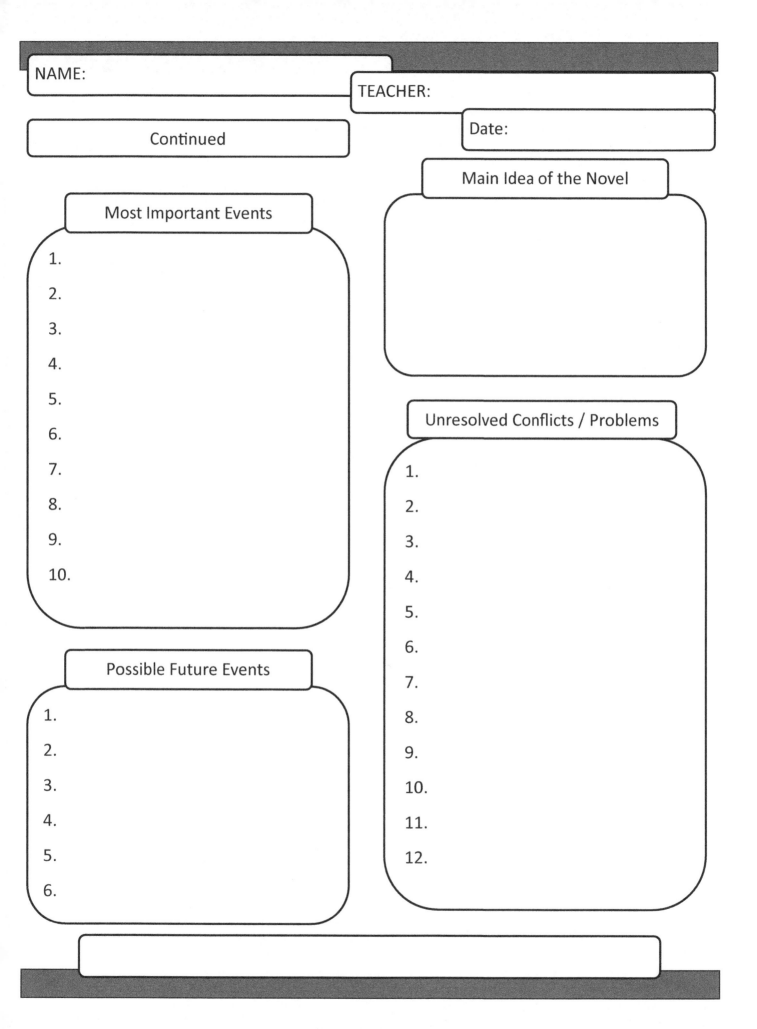

Made in United States
North Haven, CT
23 September 2023

41892452R00037